Round Table Geometry

by Elena Dworkin Wright
and
Susan Shapero

30 Activities to Connect Math and Literature related to

Sir Cumference and the First Round Table

Sir Cumference and the Dragon of Pi

Sir Cumference and the Great Knight of Angleland

Sir Cumference and the Sword in the Cone

Sir Cumference and the Isle of Immeter

by Cindy Neuschwander, illustrated by Wayne Geehan

Publisher: Charlesbridge Publishing
85 Main Street, Watertown, MA 02472

Printed in the United States of America

ISBN-13: 978-1-57091-155-2
ISBN-10: 1-57091-155-X

10 9 8

 Charlesbridge

TABLE OF CONTENTS

Making a Story Map 3

Interpersonal Activities: Puppet Show, Castle, and Dubbing 4-5

Shapes and Basic Operations 6-7

Board Game: Race to the Castle 8-9

Tangrams and Other Shape Activities 10-11

Shape Crossword and Cross-number Activities 12

Fractions: Coat-of-Arms and Armorial 13-15

Farm Fractions and Fraction Graphs 16-17

Graphing: Market Day Money 18-19

Matching, Measuring, and Marching in Hats 20-21

Measuring Diameter and Circumference 22-23

Measuring Area, Perimeter, and Length 24-25

A Kingdom of Triangles and Magic Triangles 26-27

Mazes, Secret Codes, and Rhythm Toss 28-31

Related Reading 32

INTEGRATING MATH, LITERATURE, AND MULTIPLE INTELLIGENCES

This book reinforces geometric concepts and makes a connection between literature and mathematics. The artwork and story references relate to *Sir Cumference and the First Round Table: A Math Adventure* by Cindy Neuschwander. The story shows characters using different strategies to solve a problem. Use the story map on page 3 to help students analyze the plot of the book.

PROBLEM SOLVING

The problem-solving strategies used in *Sir Cumference and the First Round Table* are applied in activities throughout this book. They include drawing a picture, considering alternatives, looking at other designs and solutions in nature, and analyzing outcomes.

Critical thinking strategies include observing, classifying, sequencing, and discovering relationships. The activities involve students in using visual/spatial, logical/mathematical, bodily/kinesthetic, verbal/linguistic, musical/rhythmic, interpersonal, and intrapersonal intelligences. The levels of difficulty within each activity allow for a wide range of student performance levels, strengths, and interests.

MAKING A STORY MAP: Answer the questions to make a story map of *Sir Cumference and the First Round Table: A Math Adventure.*

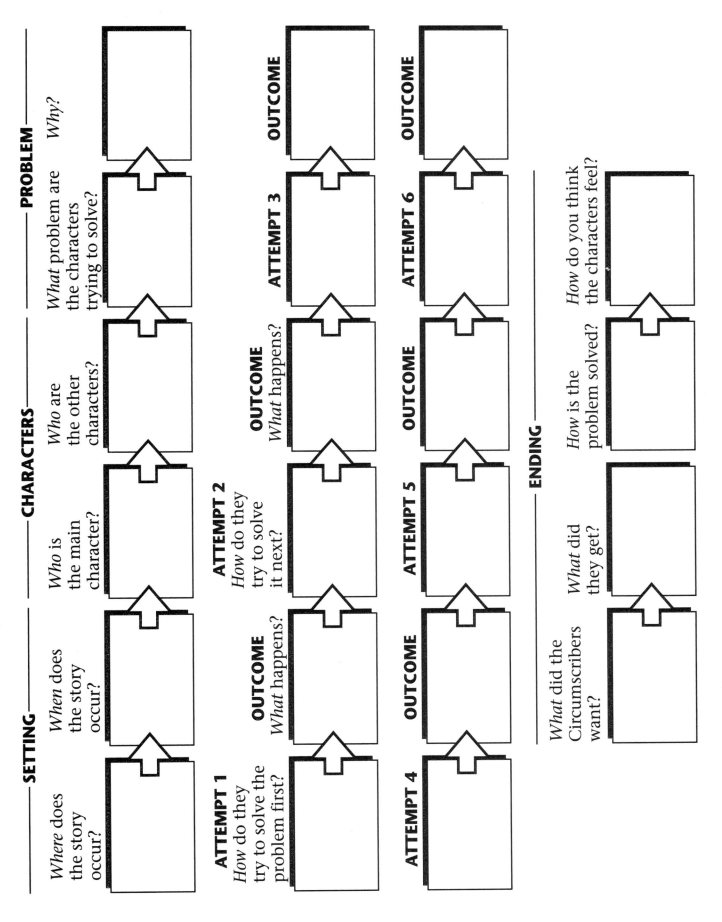

Putting on a Puppet Show

Hand out copies of **page 5**. Have the students cut out the puppets and tape them to sticks to act out a scene from the story, *Sir Cumference and the First Round Table: A Math Adventure*. Help them think of a song that can be adapted to end the show, for example, "Here We Go 'Round the Mulberry Bush," could become "Here We Go 'Round King Arthur's Table."

Building a Castle

Ask the students to name the parts of a castle: towers, turrets, walls, gate, moat, and drawbridge. Suggest some new vocabulary, such as the **keep** (strongest and most secure tower), the **wall walk** (walkway along the inside of the high walls), and the **portcullis** (the iron gate that could be lowered to block the entrance).

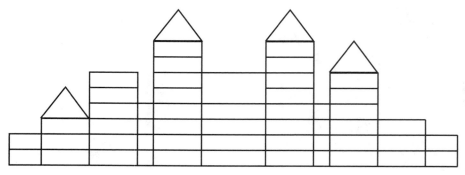

Have students work in small groups to build a castle in which to stage their puppet show. Students might build the castle of blocks. Older students might construct their own cubes by tracing the template on page 7.

I Dub Thee

Explain that, in medieval England, a seven-year-old child could become a **page** who would serve in the castle learning about proper behavior, and how to ride and tend horses. At age 14, a page could become a **squire**, tending a knight's horses, weapons, and armor.

If a squire was brave, he could be knighted by the king. The king would name the knight as he tapped first one of the knight's shoulders and then the other.

Have pairs of students choose a number from 1 to 15. Ask them to write 2 combinations of numbers that equal their sum. Each student chooses one combination and knights his or her partner, saying, "I dub thee Sir Seven," while tapping three times on one shoulder and four on the other.

Radius

Sir Cumference

Geo of Metry

King Arthur

Lady Di of Ameter

Cut out the people and tape them to sticks. Use them for a Sir Cumference show.

SHAPES AND BASIC OPERATIONS

Which Side?

Have students form groups of four. Give each group a copy of **page 7**. Have students cut out the figures and decide how to fold them to form a pair of dice. Explain that they may tape the tabs onto the outside of the cube.

Hold up one of the dice with only one side showing. Have the students look at their own dice to explain on which side a particular number of dots may be found. For example, if two dots are shown on the front, which side has four dots? Is it the top, bottom, back, left, or right side?

Odd or Even?

Have the students throw two dice and add the scores. Have them make 20 throws and record their results in a table like the one below:

First Die	+ Second Die	=	Odd or Even?
1	6	7	odd
2	2	4	even
3	4	7	odd
2	3	5	odd
4	2	6	even

Have the students think about what rules they can make from their results. What happened when they added two even numbers, two odd numbers, and an odd and an even number? On the chalkboard, draw a table like the one below to record their rules.

+	Odd	Even
Odd	(Even)	(Odd)
Even	(Odd)	(Even)

Race to the Castle

Have groups of 2-4 students use their dice to play the board game on pages 8 and 9.

Cut out the shapes. Fold each one along the dotted lines. Keep the number dots on the outside. Fold the tabs and tape them over the outside.

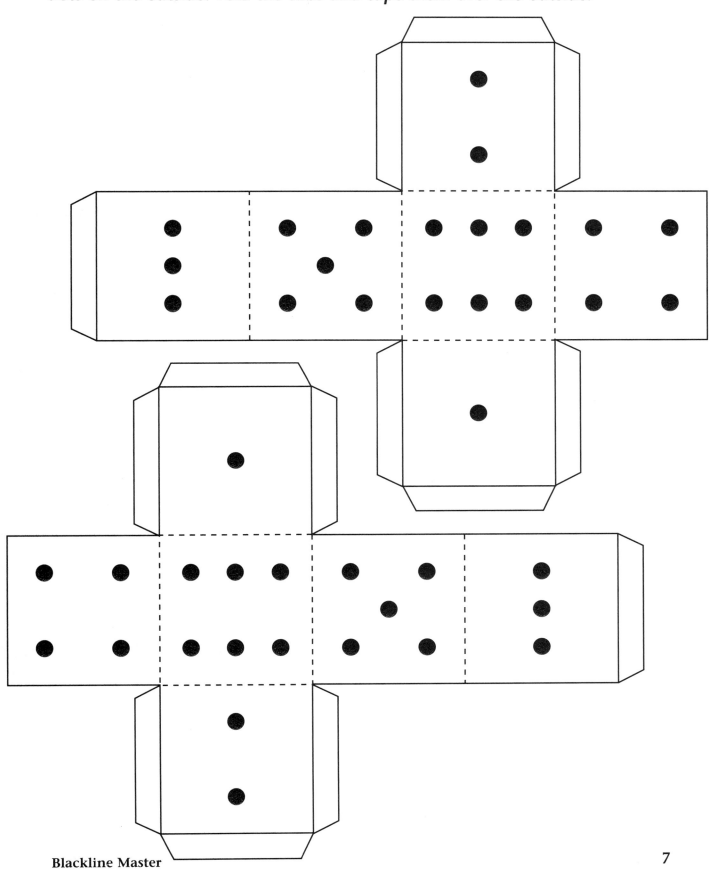

RACE to the CASTLE

Win tournament, go to next circle.

Moat overflows. Lose 1 turn.

M to n parallelo

Stop for drink. Lose 1 turn.

Help build round table. Move ahead 2.

Have tea with Lady Di. Lose 1 turn.

Round Table! Go to castle.

FINISH

START

Move to next triangle.

Dragons ahead. Lose 1 turn.

Hide from circumscribers. Move to next square.

MARKET

Lost in the forest. Lose 1 turn.

...ster gives ...g directions. ...Go back ...o market.

Watch jester juggle. Lose 1 turn.

Go back 3.

Race to the Castle

Groups of 2-4 players roll dice and move the number shown. Other games: subtract, multiply, or divide the two numbers rolled on the dice for each move.

TANGRAM STRATEGIES

Hand out copies of **page 11** and have each student cut out the seven tangram pieces. Give the following directions.

1. Put the parallelogram in front of you. Use the two small triangles to construct another parallelogram on top of it.

2. Use the parallelogram and the 2 small triangles to make a rectangle.

3. Use the parallelogram and the 2 small triangles to make a large triangle.

4. Put one of the large triangles in front of you. Use three different combinations of smaller pieces to make a triangle that is just like it.

5. Put the 2 largest triangles together to make a square. Take the remaining 5 pieces and arrange them to form another square of the same size. Put the 2 squares together to make a rectangle.

6. Ask the students to make the animals in Camelot. Have them put the pieces together to form the bird, the rabbit, and the cat shown on page 11.

7. Have students use the tangram pieces to make other animals.

Have students discuss how they solved the problems. Elicit strategies they found useful, such as flipping or rotating the pieces.

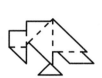 

SHAPE CROSSWORDS AND CROSS-NUMBERS

Hand out copies of the puzzles on **page 12**. Completed puzzles will look like the ones below.

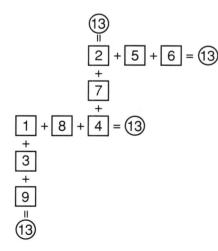 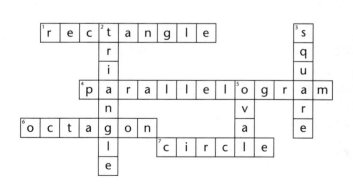

Cut out the large rectangle shape below. Carefully cut along the lines in the rectangle to make seven separate pieces. Then use the pieces to make the three animals.

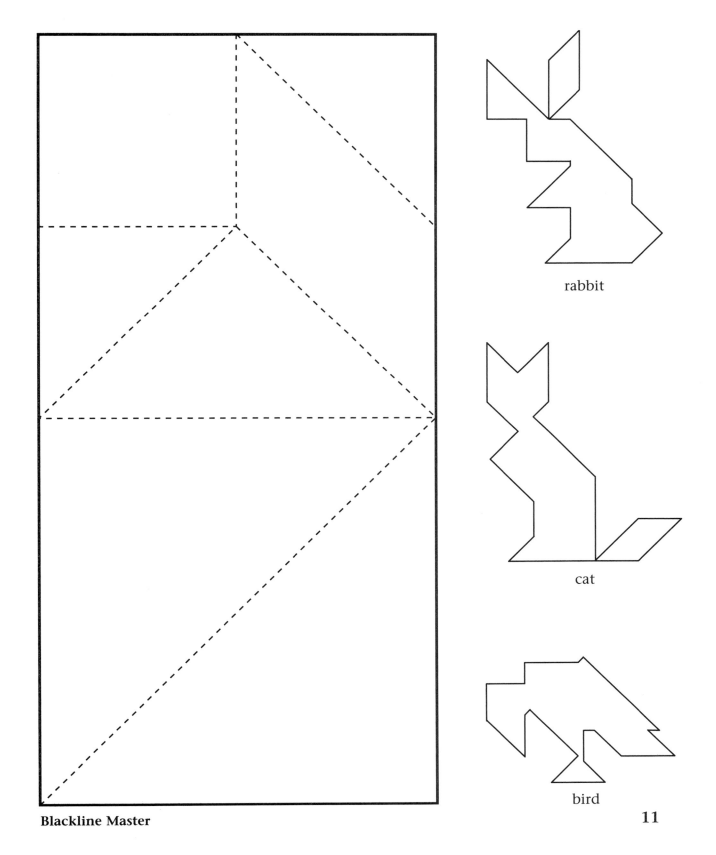

rabbit

cat

bird

Write the name of each shape in the puzzle.

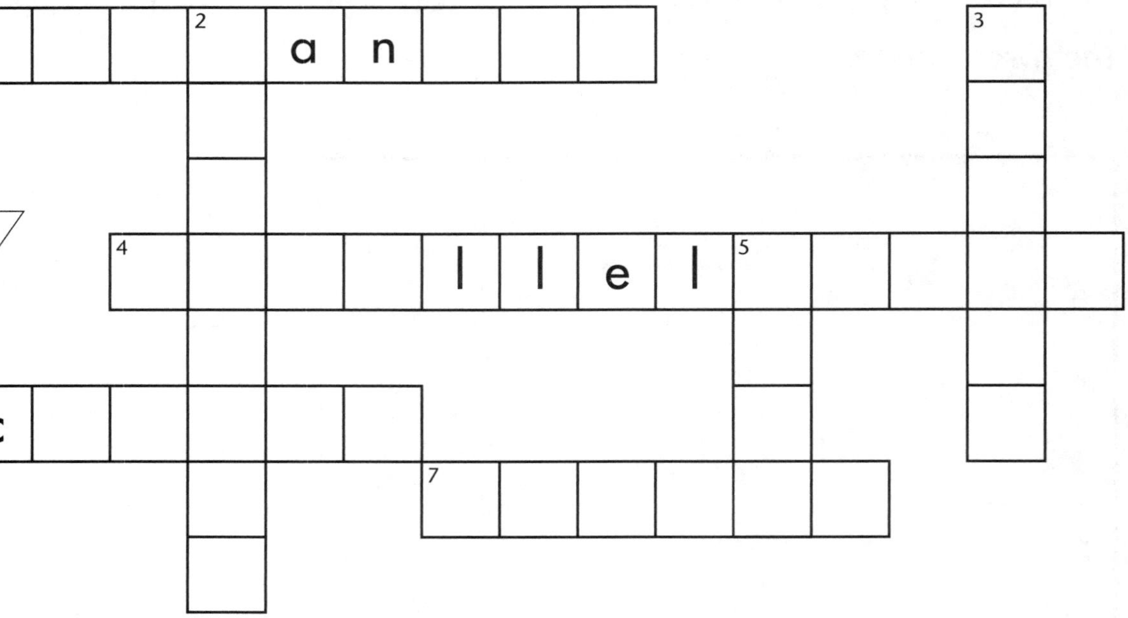

Across
1. ▱
4. 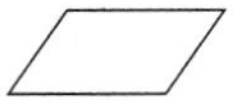 ▱
6.  ⬡
7. ○

Down
2. 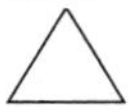 △
3. 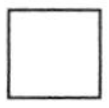 □
5.  ⬭

In the crossword grid:
1. _ _ _ 2._ **a n** _ _ _   3._
4. _ _ _ **l l e l** 5._ _ _ _ _
6. _ **c** _ _ _
7._ _ _ _ _

········· **CROSS-NUMBERS** ·········

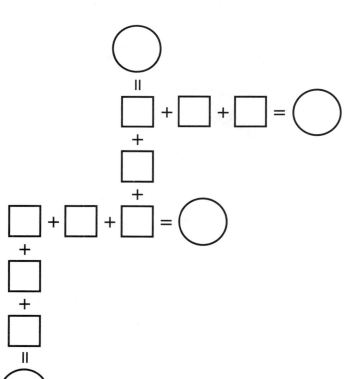

Count the letters in the longest word in the crossword puzzle. This is the lucky number. Write it in each circle. In the boxes, use the numbers 1 to 9 to add up to the lucky number. Use each number only once.

Blackline Master

Designing a Coat-of-Arms

Ask students what they know about a **coat-of-arms**. A knight had a coat-of-arms to wear on his shield and flag to show everyone that he was a knight and followed a strict code of behavior — he was brave, loyal, and generous.

Explain that the background design of a knight's shield was called the *field* and the figures on it were called *charges*.

Hand out copies of **pages 14 and 15**. Have students identify fields that are divided into halves, thirds, fourths, and sixths.

Note: The fields are divided into parts of equal area. You might have students divide rectangles and squares into equal fractional areas to make large shields.

Draw one of the fields on the board and write a color name in each section. Have students write what fraction of the field each color covers. For example, if the 3 sections of the field were blue, green, and red, they would write:

blue = 1/3,
green = 1/3,
red = 1/3.

blue = 2/3
red = 1/3

Erase the colors and relabel two of the parts blue and one part red. Ask the students to tell you what fraction each color represents.

Ask the students to design the coat-of-arms they would carry if they were medieval knights. Ask them to choose and cut out charges to fit on a field. Have volunteers explain what their designs represent.

Making a Fraction Armorial

Explain that a book called an **armorial** was the official record of each knight's coat-of-arms. Knights had to make sure that each design was different so they could identify each other on the battlefield when they were wearing helmets. They recorded all the designs in armorials.

Have students display their completed coat-of-arms designs on a bulletin board as a Fraction Armorial. Have them label their designs by the fractions. For example, if Kim chose the quartered field, 2 suns, a castle, and a unicorn, she would write 1/2 suns, 1/4 castle, 1/4 unicorn.

Each student might make a large copy of his or her field on colored construction paper with a strip of paper taped to the back as a handle. They can carry these shields during the procession. (See page 20.)

FIELDS FOR A COAT-OF-ARMS

Choose a field. Color each section and label the fractions.

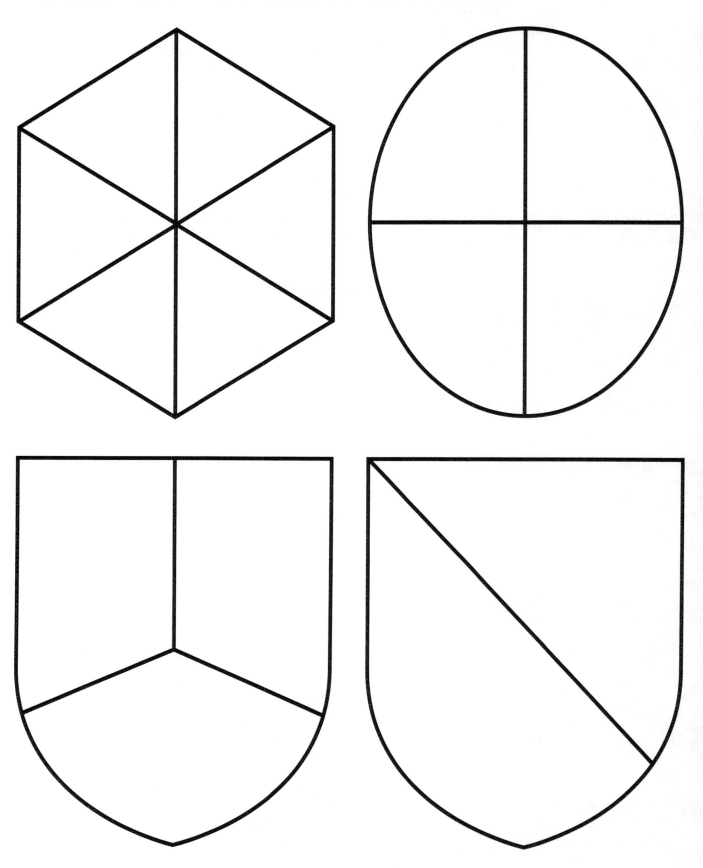

CHARGES TO GO ON A COAT-OF-ARMS

Choose your charges and cut them out. Paste one on each part of your field.

FARM FRACTIONS

Discuss how people in medieval Europe relied on their land for food, clothing, and shelter. Have students suggest some ways the land provided each. Hand out copies of **page 17** and have students divide the parcels of land into equal sections. Give the students fraction tiles in different shapes. Have them show how they would divide the parcels of land. Ask them to find three ways to solve problems 1 and 2 and two ways to solve problem 5.

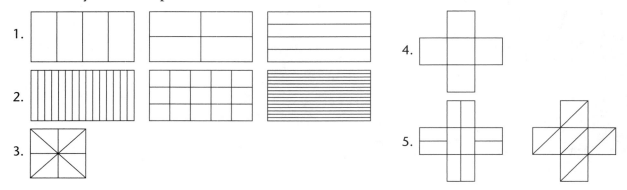

FRACTION GRAPH PICTURES

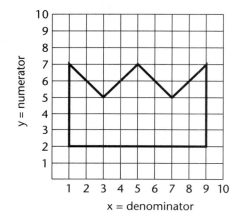

Hand out graph paper. Have students measure and draw lines to form a 10 x 10 square box. Have students label the x-axis **denominator**, the y-axis **numerator,** and number the axes from 0 to 10. Show them how to plot the fractions on a graph. To graph 2/1, count up 2 squares and over 1 square. Draw the point on the graph. Have them connect the points to draw a picture of something every king needs.

2/1   7/1   5/3   7/5   5/7   7/9   2/9

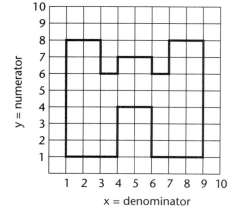

Help students plot the fractions on another 10 x 10 square graph to find a home for a round table.

1/1   8/1   8/3   6/3   6/4   7/4

7/6   6/6   6/7   8/7   8/9

1/9   1/6   4/6   4/4   1/4

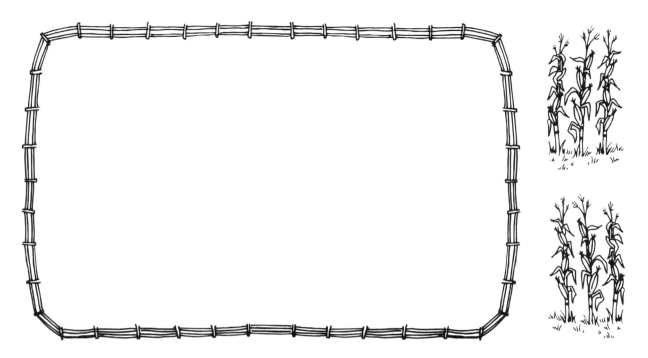

1. Find a way to plant equal areas of oats, barley, corn, and wheat.
2. Find a way to divide this land into 15 equal parts.

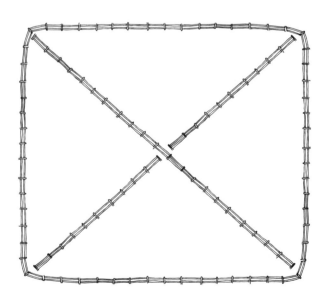

3. Help Lady Di plant mint, thyme, fennel, parsley, sage, rosemary, basil, and chives in equal sections of her garden.

4. Make equal grazing land for cows, horses, sheep, goats, and oxen.

5. Divide the land equally for ten animals.

GRAPHING: MARKET DAY MONEY

Market Day Bar Graph

Explain how, in medieval Europe, people from the countryside set up shops outside the castle to sell or trade goods. Brainstorm a list of occupations for the people in the marketplace, such as tinker, blacksmith, cook, fishmonger, cooper (barrel-maker), and potter. Write the list on the board.

Elicit some of the types of goods they might sell, such as fresh produce, herbs, grains, cheese, fish, barrels, brooms, pots, livestock, leather, and wool. Write the list of goods on the chalkboard and have the students assign a price for each (in whole dollars for first grade). Ask each student to draw a product and write its price on it.

Give half of the students $10 each in play money to spend. Have the other students set up shops to sell the goods, keep a log of what was sold, and compute the total sales. After the market, hand out copies of the graph on **page 19**.

Make a chart on the chalkboard of goods sold and amount earned by each seller.

Seller	Earnings
broom maker	$12
blacksmith	$15
cheese merchant	$ 9
fishmonger	$ 6
tinker	$20

Have students draw the bars on their graphs to show the amounts earned. Discuss the value of a bar graph for quickly summarizing lists of numbers.

Circle Graphs

Have 2 volunteer customers show the class their purchases. Have each volunteer write a list on the chalkboard to show how his or her money was spent. Have students who know percent convert the amounts to percentages. Write the percentages on the board.

Draw circle graphs to illustrate how each volunteer spent the $10. Have students compare the circle graphs, asking such questions as, "Who spent more on food?" or "Who bought more items?"

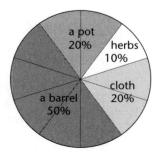

MARKET DAY GRAPH

Sales Totals

0   10   20   30   40   50   60   70   80   90   100

Sellers

MATCHING, MEASURING, AND MARCHING IN HATS

Put the Hats on their Owners

Discuss the kinds of headgear worn by the characters in *Sir Cumference and the First Round Table*. Discuss the purpose of a helmet for a knight or a crown for a king. Hand out copies of **page 21**. The students may draw lines between the hats and the people who wear them, or they may cut out the hats and paste each hat on a character with a matching sum.

Make a Crown, Lady's Hat, or a Helmet

Have students measure and record the size of their heads. Hand out 11- by 17-inch construction paper and have students measure and cut out strips that are four inches high and two inches longer than the circumference of their heads. Have them measure two inches from the long edge to draw a line down the center of the strip.

Ask them to make a dot every two inches along the line and along the top of the strip. Have them connect the dots.

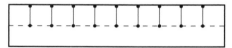

Have them draw triangles by connecting every other dot along the outside edge to two dots on the center line. Students can cut along these lines to form the points of a crown.

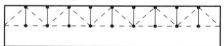

For a lady's hat, students can cut the points to make a scalloped top.

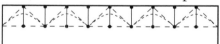

For a helmet, have students cut another strip of paper two inches wide. The length should be the diameter of the circle plus nine inches. They tape this strip across the circle so that one end hangs down 4 inches in the front as a nose guard.

March in a Procession

Students can wear their hats and carry their shields as they march in a circular procession to medieval music such as *Greensleeves*. Have students step and count time to the rhythm of the music. They might also play percussion instruments. You might refer to the following resources for other songs from this period:

Video - *Discovering the Music of the Middle Ages*
CD - *Forgotten Provence: Music Making in the South of France*
Book and Audiocassette - *Welcome in the Spring: Morris and Sword Dances for Children*

PUT THE HATS ON THEIR OWNERS

Do the math problems. Cut out each hat and paste it on the person with the same answer.

MEASURING DIAMETER AND CIRCUMFERENCE

Discovering Pi

Draw a circle on the chalkboard and have the students identify its parts. Write in the name of each part the students identify: circumference, diameter, and radius.

Draw on the chalkboard 3 progressively larger circles with the diameter lines marked. Have students draw 3 circles like those on the board. Have students use string to measure the diameter of the smallest circle. Ask them to find how many diameter lengths of string it takes to measure the circumference of the same circle.

Have them do the same with the middle-sized circle, and then with the largest circle. Ask students to discover how many diameter lengths it takes to measure these circles.

Hand out copies of **page 23** and supply round objects for students to measure: cans, flower pots, paper plates, etc.

Discuss the results of the students' measurements. Elicit from them the relationship between the diameter of each circle and its circumference. Point out that **pi** is the term used to denote this relationship: the circumference is slightly more than three times the diameter of the circle, 3.14159265.

Circle Magic

Demonstrate how to push a quarter through a dime-sized hole. Trace a dime to make a circle in the middle of an index card. Cut out the circle. Push a quarter through the hole without tearing the card by folding the card along the diameter of the hole.

By bending the card, the hole becomes a different shape with a larger diameter. It becomes an ellipse. Pass around two or three index cards with pre-cut holes so students can try the trick.

Target Practice

Draw a target on the chalkboard like the one below.

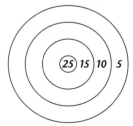

Pose the following type of problem for the students to solve. Sir Cumference shot 5 arrows and hit the target each time. He scored 45 points in all. If his arrows hit 3 different numbers, what were his 5 scores? (Answer: 15, 10, 10, 5, and 5)

MEASURING DIAMETER AND CIRCUMFERENCE

Is the following statement true or false?

The circumference of a circle is approximately three times greater than its diameter.

How to test this statement:

1. *Choose three round objects of different sizes.*

2. *Measure across the middle (diameter) with a ruler.*

3. *Measure around the object (circumference).*

Object	Circumference	Diameter	T or F
a.			
b.			
c.			

4. *Record your results.*

5. *Check to see how many times you can add the diameter and come closest to the circumference. Use a calculator.*

6. *What conclusions can you make?*

MEASURING AREA, PERIMETER, AND LENGTH

Discuss the concept of area — the number of square units in a shape, and perimeter — the outer boundary of a shape. Elicit appropriate square units to measure each of the following: a piece of paper, a room, a kingdom. Draw a 5 by 5 square grid on the chalkboard. Have students find the area and perimeter of the square.

Hand out copies of **page 25** and have students count the squares of the area and the edges of the perimeter of each table shape.

L	p = 20	a = 9	T	p = 18	a = 8	C	p = 20	a = 9
F	p = 22	a = 10	I	p = 12	a = 5	S	p = 24	a = 11
E	p = 22	a = 10	H	p = 16	a = 7	J	p = 16	a = 7

Table Design Perimeters

Have students measure and cut an 8-inch by 10-inch rectangle from a piece of construction paper. Ask them to draw a diagonal line on it as shown below. Have them cut along the diagonal to make 2 triangles. Ask students to explore all they ways they can put the 2 triangles together to make other shapes such as the ones below.

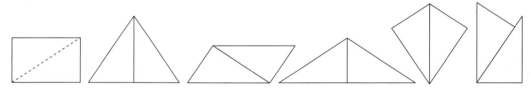

Have them measure the perimeter of each shape to find which table shape would seat more people if each inch equals a foot and each person requires four feet of perimeter.

The Road is Long

Give each student a piece of graph paper to draw a model of Sherwood Forest. Read the following aloud.

Sherwood Forest is a square. Each side is 10 miles long. A road starts at the exact center of the forest and makes a lot of turns. Draw the road. It goes 1 mile north, then 2 miles west, 3 miles south, 4 miles east, 5 miles north, 6 miles west, 7 miles south, 8 miles east, and north until it reaches the edge of the forest. On which side does the road reach the edge of the forest? How many miles long is it?

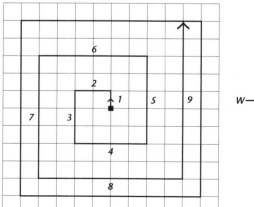

The students drawings should look like the one to the left. The road is 1+2+3+4+5+6+7+8+9=45 miles long, and reaches the north edge of the forest.

24

Find the perimeter of each table shape by counting the outside edges of all the squares in each figure. Find the area by counting the squares.

Perimeter = _____ cm.

Perimeter = _____ cm.

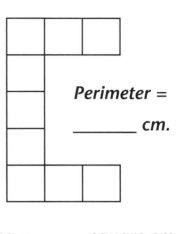

Perimeter = _____ cm.

Area = _____ square cm.

Area = _____ square cm.

Area = _____ square cm.

Perimeter = _____ cm.

Perimeter = _____ cm.

Perimeter = _____ cm.

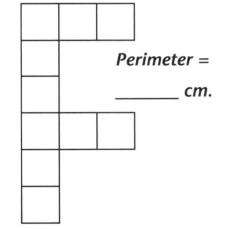

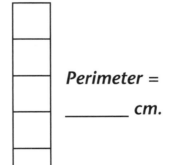

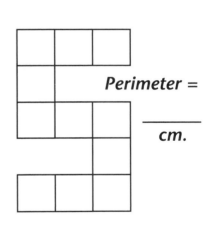

Area = _____ square cm.

Area = _____ square cm.

Area = _____ square cm.

Perimeter = _____ cm.

Perimeter = _____ cm.

Perimeter = _____ cm.

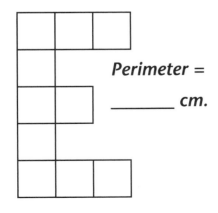

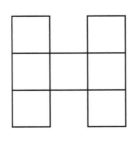

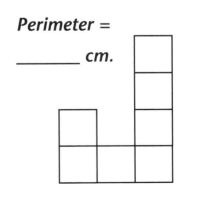

Perimeter = _____ cm.

Area = _____ square cm.

Area = _____ square cm.

Area = _____ square cm.

A KINGDOM OF TRIANGLES

Hand out copies of **page 27**. Explain that after the Circumscribers measured their kingdom, they found it was shaped like a star. They want to plant five types of flowers in their kingdom. Have the students outline the 5 large and 5 small triangles in the star to show the Circumscribers' options. Then have them use five colors to outline the five bigger triangles.

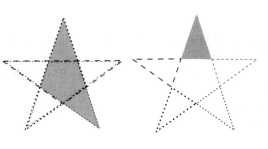

Cut a Five-Pointed Star

Each student will need scissors and a piece of 8 1/2- by 11-inch colored paper to make this star. Demonstrate the following steps:

1. Hold the paper sideways and fold it in half. Place the folded edge on the left.

2. Fold the bottom left corner up to the middle of the top edge.

3. Fold the top left corner down.

4. Bring the top left folded edge down to the bottom folded edge.

5. Measure a triangle that is 4 inches along the bottom edge and 2 inches along the left side.

6. Cut off the triangle and unfold your star.

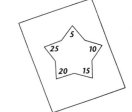

Have younger students write numerals counting by fives in each point of the star. Older students can write fives multiplication facts. String their stars into a constellation mobile.

Magic Triangles

Draw the diagram on the right on the chalkboard. Ask students how to use the numbers from 1 to 9 so that the sum along each side is 20.

Solution:
5+4+2+9=20
5+6+8+1=20
1+3+7+9=20

Have them draw a similar diagram of 3 boxes on each side of the triangle and use the numbers 1 through 6 to add up to 9.

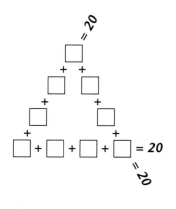

How many triangles can you find in this star? Cut out the 2 triangles on the bottom of this page. Trace five little triangles in the star. Trace five bigger triangles in the star. Use a different color to outline each of the bigger triangles.

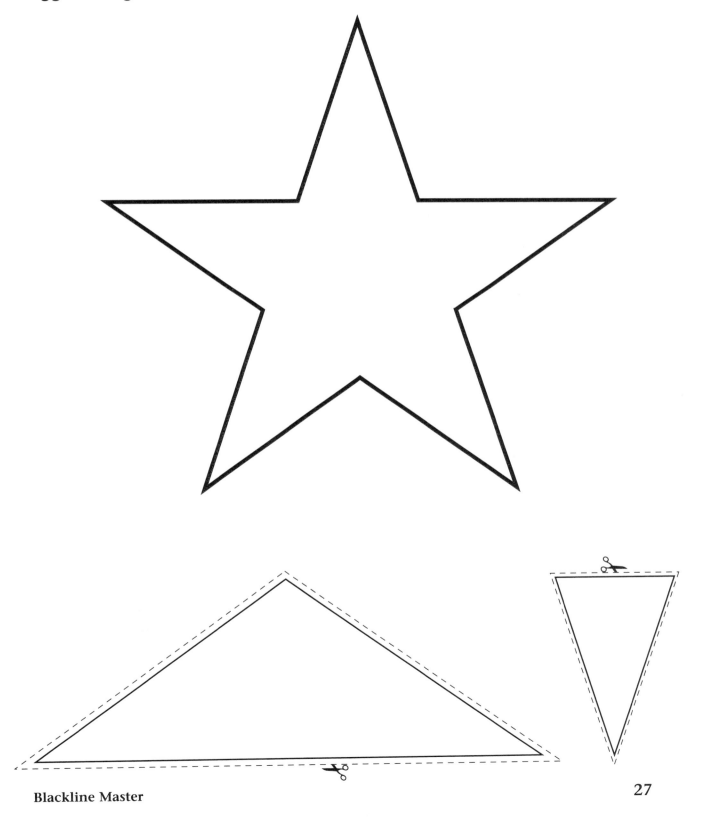

Leaving the Castle Maze

Have students solve the addition and subtraction problems on **page 29** to find the way out of the castle.

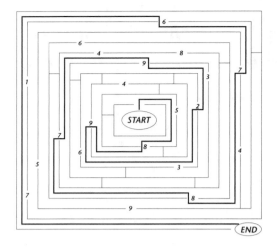

Chess Code

Point out that board games like chess have been played for thousands of years and were popular in medieval England. Have students describe the pieces on the chessboard and discuss which ones could represent characters and settings from the story *Sir Cumference and the First Round Table: A Math Adventure.*

On the chalkboard draw the grid on the right. Explain that, to read the code, students will find the numbers of the column and row for each letter. Demonstrate how to decode a word. For example, K is in row 3 and column 1, so the number for K is 31. The code for the word knight would be 31-34-24-22-23-45.

	1	2	3	4	5
1	A	B	C	D	E
2	F	G	H	I	J
3	K	L	M	N	O
4	P	Q	R	S	T
5	U	V	W	X	Y/Z

Write the following problem on the chalkboard and have students decode the solution:

This is one shape Geo didn't build. It is the name of a famous building in Washington, D.C.

41-15-34-45-11-22-35-34   The shape is a _____ .

You may want to have students continue their study of shapes by measuring pentagons or doing the circle and pentagon activity below.

Circle Code

Hand out copies of **page 30**. Explain that in King Arthur's day, people used Roman numerals to count. Have students translate each sequence of Arabic numerals to the same sequence in Roman numerals. They can read the letters beneath each sequence to decode each word in the message: *Radius got around the problem.* Students may enjoy writing other secret messages about the story to share with their families.

Rhythm Toss

Have students cut out the circles on **page 31**, then work with other students to tape together the flaps of 12 shapes into a ball. Ask students what the shape of each surface is (a pentagon).

LEAVING THE CASTLE MAZE

Help Radius find his way out of King Arthur's castle. Solve each problem.
Each answer is a clue to which door to enter.

CLUES

a. 11 - 3 = ☐   e. 24 - 17 = ☐

b. 7 + 2 = ☐   f. 4 + 4 = ☐

c. 30 - 28 = ☐   g. 22 - 15 = ☐

d. 3 + 6 = ☐   h. 10 + 4 = ☐

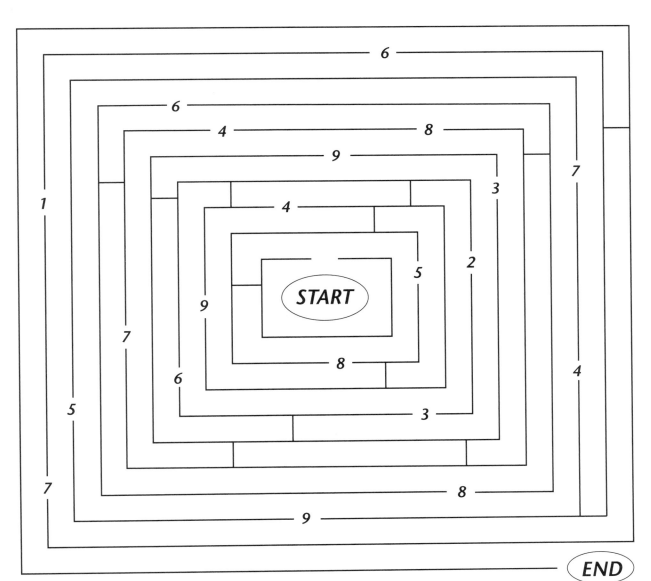

Cut out the small wheel. Put the small wheel inside of the big wheel. Turn the small wheel so the Roman numeral XXV is above the letter R. XXV = 25. Decode the rest of the message.

25	8	11	16	2	26

14	22	1

8	25	22	2	21	11

1	15	12

23	25	22	9	19	12	20

30

Radius likes to play catch with his friends. Follow the directions to make a ball like his. To play, walk in a circle, saying the following rhyme, and tossing the ball on the underlined word.

> "We have a ball as good as <u>gold</u>.
> We toss it round like knights so <u>bold</u>."

1. Cut out the circles.
2. Fold up the flaps.
3. With three other students, tape together the flaps of 12 pentagons to make a ball.

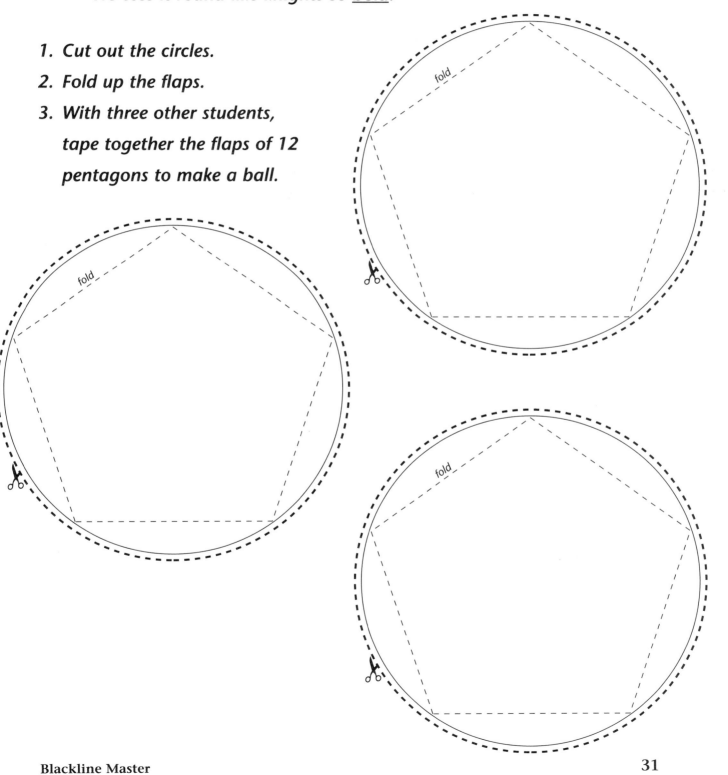

RELATED READING

The following is a list of other books about knights and the Middle Ages that your students may enjoy. Many of the activities in this book can be adapted to accompany these stories as well.

Fiction

Carrick, Donald. *Harold and the Giant Knight*. Clarion. 1982.

Christelow, Eileen. *Henry and the Dragon*. Clarion. 1984.

De Paola, Tomie. *The Knight and the Dragon*. Putnam. 1980.

Gerrard, Roy. *Sir Cedric*. Farrar Straus Giroux. 1984.

Hastings, Selina. *Sir Gawain and the Loathly Lady*. Lothrop, Lee & Shepard Books. 1985.

Hodges, Margaret. *The Kitchen Knight: A Tale of King Arthur*. Holiday House. 1990.

Hunter, Mollie. *Knight of the Golden Plain*. Harper & Row. 1983.

Lasker, Joe. *A Tournament of Knights*. T.Y. Crowell. 1986.

McAllister, Angela. *Battle of Sir Cob and Sir Filbert*. Clarkson N. Potter. 1991.

McCaughrean, Geraldine. *Saint George and the Dragon*. Doubleday. 1989.

Morpurgo, Michael. *Arthur, High King of Britain*. Harcourt Brace. 1995.

O'Connor, Jane. *Sir Small and the Dragonfly*. Random House. 1988.

San Souci, Robert D. *Young Guinevere*. Doubleday. 1993.

Scieszka, Jon. *Knights of the Kitchen Table*. Puffin. 1993.

Service, Pamela. *The Wizard of Wind and Rock*. Antheneum. 1990.

White, T.H. *The Sword in the Stone*. Philomel. 1993.

Non-fiction

Aliki. *A Medieval Feast*. Harper Collins. 1983.

Clare, John D. *Knights in Armor*. Harcourt Brace Jovanovich. 1992.

Crawford, Sue. *Lands of Legend*. Bookwright Press. 1989.

Gravett, Christopher. *The Knight's Handbook: How to Become a Champion in Shining Armor*. Cobblehill. 1997.

Honan, Linda. *Picture the Middle Ages*. Golden Owl. 1994.

Howarth, Sarah. *The Middle Ages*. Viking. 1993.

Hunt, Jonathan. *Illuminations*. Aladdin Books. 1993.

Oakes, Catherine. *Exploring the Past: The Middle Ages*. Harcourt. 1989.

Ragache, Gilles. *Myths and Legends of Dragons*. Marshall Cavendish. 1991.

Sancha, Selena. *Crafts and Trade in the Middle Ages*. HarperCollins. 1989.

Steele, Philip. *Castles*. Kingfisher. 1995.